Pathways to Devotion IV
By Linda McBurney-Gunhouse

Published by:
Creative Focus Publishing
Winnipeg Beach, Manitoba,
Canada

Cover Artwork by Linda McBurney-Gunhouse
ISBN: 978-1-928071-16-7

Copyright © 2007 by Linda McBurney-Gunhouse
All Rights Reserved.
R3

Published by:
Creative Focus Publishing
Box 704
Winnipeg Beach, Manitoba
R0C 3G0 CANADA

Please visit our website:
www.creativefocus.ca

Contact us at:
info@creativefocus.ca

All Scripture is taken from the King James Version of the Bible, unless otherwise stated.

A Note from the Author

Pathways to Devotion IV, is the fourth in a series of devotional books, offering new and insightful inspirational reflections to encourage you as you journey along through life's many interesting pathways. Backed by spiritual themes, you'll find quotes from the Bible in each reflection, designed to uplift, strengthen and create pause for thought.

Many of the reflections are little stories of interesting, insightful and even miraculous things that have happened to me through the years. Underlying it all is a faith in a loving God who promises He will be with us throughout all the circumstances of life. At the end of each reflection, is a section called Application. Here, you are given a guideline for further Scripture reading, prayer and further reflection. I invite you to use this book as a companion to your Bible and treat it as either a daily devotional book, or use it as a guideline for small Bible study groups. I leave you with one of my favourite passages of Scripture:

Psalm 23:1-3,6

The LORD is my shepherd; I shall not want. He maketh me to lie down in green pastures: he leadeth me beside the still waters. He restoreth my soul: he leadeth me in the paths of righteousness for his name's sake. Surely goodness and mercy shall follow me all the days of my life: and I will dwell in the house of the LORD forever.

Linda McBurney-Gunhouse
Winnipeg Beach, MB
Canada

Contents

Day 1 - Doing an Undo 1
Day 2 - Giftings or Grace? 3
Day 3 - Getting Along 5
Day 4 - Grace or Convenience? 7
Day 5 - Looks Can Be Deceiving 9
Day 6 - Beauty in Chaos 11
Day 7 - The Discipline of Self 13
Day 8 - Our Father's Business 15
Day 9 - Faith in Motion 17
Day 10 - Free-Fall 19
Day 11 - Lowly in Heart 21
Day 12 - Ease or Unease? 23
Day 13 - Coincidence or Providence? 25
Day 14 - In the Moment 27
Day 15 - Weight Loss by Prayer 29
Day 16 - Walking Off The Job 31
Day 17 - Does God Care? 33
Day 18 - Helping Hands 35
Day 19 - Sounds in the Night 37
Day 20 - After Retirement? 39
Day 21 - The Wrong Fit 41
Day 22 - Righting Wrongs 43
Day 23 - An Aging Population 45
Day 24 - True Freedom 47
Day 25 - Reliable Sources 49
Day 26 - Earthen Vessels 51
Day 27 - Passing a Test 53
Day 28 - Sharing Good News 55
Day 29 - A True Definition 57
Day 30 - Weather-Wise 59
An Invitation for Salvation 61
About the Author 62
Other Titles 64

This book is lovingly dedicated to my mother, Pauline E. (Bonk) McBurney, who is such an inspiration to me and whose name is mentioned in this and all my other devotional books. May the Lord bless her abundantly as she continues to faithfully go about, joyfully doing her heavenly Father's work.

Day 1 - <u>Doing an Undo</u>

And you, being dead in your sins and the uncircumcision of your flesh, hath he quickened together with him, having forgiven you all trespasses; Blotting out the handwriting of ordinances that was against us, which was contrary to us, and took it out of the way, nailing it to his cross; Colossians 2:13-14

As a writer and artist, I use my computer almost on a daily basis to get my work done. Often when I am working with my photos or creating a new artistic design, I experiment with different effects in my graphics programs to find the best layout or I start from scratch and draw a new picture. One of the functions I use all the time is the "undo" command. This means that if I make a mistake while painting or drawing, or if I don't like a particular effect, I can simply press the "undo" button and it takes me back a step. In fact, I can keep pressing it until I go back to the original picture. I am so thankful for this function and am sure it was inspired by God to the programmers who designed it. It has saved me many a headache.

Sometimes when I am sewing, I make a mistake. This is especially true when I am sewing on a border to go around a quilt. A straight line is anything but straight since the material moves from the weight of the quilt and I have to tear it out and start all over again (sometimes several times until it is straight). Since I am so used to using the "undo" button on the computer, I often look for it on the sewing machine as well. Then I laugh at myself, realizing that not everything has an "undo" button. Besides, once something is sewn, it still has to be taken apart since there's no machine I know of that will erase the mistake that was made.

I believe that when God thought about creating the earth and creating man and woman, He had a perfect design in mind.

Day 1

And when everything was created, it was perfect. After each thing God created, He said to the effect, "It is good." We might not illuminated. There are billions more unseen to the human eye. Think of an evening when you stood outside and watched the Northern Lights dancing magically and mysteriously across the sky. Think of the heights of majestic mountains so high they are lost in the mist of the clouds.

To give you a better idea of how awesome God is, I'd like to share about something we read in a book that talked about the holiness of God. The author shared that in the Book of Revelation (see Rev. 4:8), it says that there are four living creatures who worship at the throne of God night and day without any rest. We wonder how they can do this, but they have a front row seat in God's marvellous presence and every time God reveals something more about Himself, they bow and worship. It is so awesome, they cry out, "Holy, Holy, Holy." In response to this, the Bible says that 24 elders fall down before God, worship Him and throw their crowns before God's throne. God is a holy God, so much so, that we can only wonder how or why He loves us so much. In light of this, to use the word "awesome" so loosely and as part of our every day language seems more like slang and an inappropriate use of a word that only belongs to God. May we use it respectfully and often in reference to our awesome and incredible God.

Application

<u>Read</u>: Revelation 4

<u>Pray</u>: Seek God for a glimpse and a revelation of His holiness. Ask Him to help guide you in a meditation of Scripture about His awesomeness.

<u>Reflect</u>: In what ways has God revealed His holiness to you? Write about it. Then spend some quiet time meditating on Scriptures that talk about the awesomeness of God. Use a Bible concordance if you have one or borrow one from a friend.

Day 2 - <u>Giftings or Grace?</u>

And he said unto me, My grace is sufficient for thee: for my strength is made perfect in weakness. Most gladly therefore will I rather glory in my infirmities, that the power of Christ may rest upon me. 2 Corinthians 12:9

A friend once said to me that he never thought of me as a public speaker. Perhaps he thought this because the kind of work that I do is solitary and requires little people-interaction except through the course of normal daily activities, like shopping or doing business-related activities. Yet public speaking is something I've been doing since a teenager, when I first enrolled as a student in college to study journalism. In order to be a journalist you have to be able to interview people and there is no room for shyness or introversion. I believe many people who frequently perform or speak before a crowd are actually introverts at heart. I also believe that many people are called to share their giftings, even and sometimes especially if they struggle with some aspect of sharing it.

In my own situation, when I first started teaching, I thought that surely the Lord couldn't mean that He wanted me to do this as a profession, since just trying to quiet the class down was a major accomplishment, never mind actually starting the lesson where they might learn something. But I soon learned that I could never walk into a classroom without first praying and asking the Lord to be with me, guide me and show me how to reach these students. I came to realize that teaching, for me, was not so much a gifting, as it was an act of grace on God's part, since I knew I couldn't succeed without leaning heavily on Him. That is grace — leaning heavily on the Lord in any area where we are weak or perhaps even feel powerless to handle it ourselves.

Salvation is a complete work of God's grace in our lives.

Day 2

We are utterly incapable of saving ourselves. Yet, even after we're saved, we sometimes keep trying to live this exciting, but difficult life on our own. We forget that we are always in need of God's grace. Perhaps this is why He sometimes calls us to do things that are so contrary to our nature, or even our personality. He wants our journey to be one filled with grace, rather than one filled with glory to ourselves where we take the credit for all our own giftings and accomplishments. Sometimes people wonder how I accomplish so many things in my life — writing books, teaching, painting, sewing, jewelry creations and more and they wonder how I can do all this. But I have learned that I need to rely on God's grace and credit Him for giving me the ability, inspiration and perseverance in spite of many setbacks and personal doubts and weaknesses. In fact, He has shown me that in order to succeed, I must lean on Him from start to finish and look to Him to accomplish His works through me.

I encourage you today — if the Lord is asking you to do something out of the ordinary, be willing to say "yes." It will be the beginning of something far more meaningful than just using your giftings — it will result in a hand-holding partnership with the Lord, discovering that His grace is all you'll ever need.

Application

<u>Read</u>: 2 Corinthians 12:1-10

<u>Pray</u>: Ask God to help you be open to experience new paths of grace in your life.

<u>Reflect</u>: What are some times when you have relied strictly on the grace of God to help you through a challenging situation? Write about it and share it.

Day 3 - <u>Getting Along</u>

For though we walk in the flesh, we do not war after the flesh: (For the weapons of our warfare are not carnal, but mighty through God to the pulling down of strongholds;) 2 Corinthians 10:3-4

Have you ever had someone say something to you that hurt you and you just couldn't seem to get over it? I am sure we all have. In one week, I had three people upset with me for the way that I said things, even though my intent was good and I didn't realize I had offended them. Family members especially seem to hurt us more than others because we are close to them and we're supposed to get along with them. We expect them to love us and forgive our short-comings, over-look our faults and accept us for who we are, mistakes and all. For me, I find that when I am worn out, over-tired and stressed in some way, I will be less tolerant of those around me and flare-ups sometimes occur. Holidays especially can be one of the most stressful times for families, since our workload increases and we are off our regular routines. It is also a time when we spend more time together than usual and expectations run much higher, whether it be clean up in the kitchen or children who do not get along. We may eat more, exercise less and get less sleep than usual.

The truth is, as long as we are involved in any kind of human relationships, we are bound to get hurt at some point in the relationship. People will let us down, and we will also disappoint them from time to time. But when we are angry with someone without a real cause or even when our anger feels justified, we take it upon ourselves to become a judge of that person, and then we feel justified when we've told him or her off feeling that the score has now been evened.

I have often wondered how to handle these unpleasant situations, especially when you can't seem to forget what someone has said or done or not done that has hurt you. In the opening verse, I believe we have the answer. Since disagreements are usually a work of the unregenerate flesh (see verses below), we must not fight back with the means of the flesh. As humbling and as difficult as it is, we need to lift up our enemies and those who we feel have wronged us, in prayer. But to fight them back is to take the path of least resistance, and will do more harm in the long run than good. The more we fight, the less victory we will have in our lives and it is certain that God cannot bless us if we harbor bad feelings of bitterness and hatred in our hearts. It is always better to try to talk it out with the person who has hurt us rather than spew our anger, for once we have said things, we cannot erase what's been said.

There is tremendous power in unity, and I believe unity is only possible through the work of the Holy Spirit in our lives. I am thankful that my mother has always encouraged me and my three siblings to get along and live in peace with one another. We may have had our disagreements, but we remain true to each other through thick and thin. We pull together in a crisis and in every celebration, laying aside our differences. This is a tremendous gift and one that we all need to strive for.

Application

Read: Galatians 5:19-26

Pray: Ask God to help you forgive those who have hurt you. Pray for them and forgive them so you an experience peace and victory in your own life.

Reflect: Are there people who have hurt you that you still haven't forgiven? Do so, and then if possible, do something or say something nice to that person to restore the relationship.

Day 4 - <u>Grace or Convenience?</u>

For the time will come when they will not endure sound doctrine; but after their own lusts shall they heap to themselves teachers, having itching ears;
2 Timothy 4:3

I remember years ago, it was quite clear when someone was doing something wrong. Black was black and white was white. There didn't seem to be as much crime as there is today. Couples didn't get a divorce and children were raised by two heterosexual parents who stayed together through every kind of difficulty. To speak out against authority was frowned upon and this included all levels of government, your teachers, your parents and anyone who was older than you (or your parent's age). If you got in trouble in school, you would also be in trouble with your parents at home. Parents recognized the need of healthy discipline in our lives, and this would pay off later in the real world, especially with regards to how we treat our boss and co-workers. It seemed we lived in a relatively safe world since we knew right from wrong and there was seldom any middle ground.

But things are different today — the lines between black and white are so blurred, people have fallen into a muddy gray compromise when it comes to morals and right living. It takes courage to speak the truth in a world where compromise is the norm. We fear that people won't like us for taking a stand when it comes to moral and spiritual issues. Few people want to stand on a moral platform and be ridiculed by others who do not want to be faced with their own moral shortcomings, yet without the knowledge of our own sin, how can we hope to be saved from the devastating effects and results that sin brings? To say nothing and do nothing is to agree that sin is okay. Surely God can't agree with this. I believe part of the problem is that we have mistaken grace for love. Although grace and the ability to accept someone in spite of their sin is part of loving someone, it is by no means the whole picture. We can show grace and mercy to everyone we meet, but what good will it do them if they feel they have done nothing wrong? They need to know that they have violated God's Word and are in great need of a Savior before grace will mean anything to them at all. I didn't realize I needed grace until I knew I had greatly sinned against God. The Holy Spirit revealed my need of grace and also revealed that He is a holy God who cannot tolerate sin. Grace could not be appreciated or even received without a knowledge of the depth of my sin and how much I needed Him in my life.

It may be convenient to turn a blind eye to sin and try to cover it all with God's grace, rather than do something about it. But this is nowhere found in Scripture. We need to be careful how we use this grace that God intends to use for His ultimate glory, and not abuse it in order to avoid the real change that must take place in our hearts. Since God entrusts us with His love, truth and grace, we need to prayerfully consider how we relate these gifts to others and not stand in the way of the work God may want to do in a person's life. May we pray for wisdom in this regard.

Application

Read: 2 Timothy 4:3-5

Pray: for the courage to speak up when necessary, and that God grants you wisdom and discernment when it comes to sharing His gifts of love, truth and grace.

Reflect: Describe a situation where God or someone else extended grace to you. How have you shown grace to others?

Day 5 - <u>Looks Can Be Deceiving</u>

While we look not at the things which are seen, but at the things which are not seen: for the things which are seen are temporal; but the things which are not seen are eternal. 2 Corinthians 4:18

When we first moved into our condo, I was anxious to make it feel like home as quickly as possible. We had never had so much space to fill. Even the upstairs bathroom seemed spacious. A store close by was selling all of their winter stock of furniture at greatly reduced prices. One day I noticed a unique towel rack that stands on a pedestal and has a shelf with two bars on the top and two bars lower down. Excited, we put it together, and then placed it in the bathroom. But I had miscalculated the size of the towel rack in proportion to the extra space in the bathroom. The towel rack was too big, so we had to take it back for a refund.

When I was a teenager and living in a rural town, there weren't many clothing stores, so we did a lot of catalogue shopping for clothes. I'd pick out a pair of jeans that looked great in the catalogue. But, similar to the towel rack, when they'd arrive I'd discover to my disappointment that they were either too big or too small, or just didn't fit properly. Other times I have gone to a restaurant and ordered something that looked good on the menu, like a special salad topped with chicken, but the chicken and the dressing were so spicy I couldn't enjoy the rest of the salad.

Many things in life are like that — they look good in the picture, but in reality they do not fit our needs. What you see is not always what you get. Spiritually, we are encouraged to view things from a completely different perspective. We are asked to see things that can't be seen with the natural eye! How is this possible? Literally, it means that once our focus is on the things of God, temporal things that we can see with the natural eye will fade into

Day 5

insignificance in comparison to the things of God. This doesn't mean we walk blindly through life; but I think it does mean we look beyond our circumstances and the temporal things of the world and look into the deeper things of God.

I believe that especially when it comes to people, we need to remember the saying: "Don't judge a book by its cover." God looks at every individual with great love and compassion, for these are the people He died for. He longs to bring each one to Himself and insure that they join Him in heaven one day. This includes ALL people, no matter what anyone has done. Do we judge people and think they wouldn't be interested in hearing about God and the Gospel message based on their appearance or mannerisms? I have found that the most unlikely people are open to hear about God and the Gospel message, and they will never forget that we shared with them. I have had co-workers tell me years later that they still remember me sharing about God with them.

God's timetable is eternal, while ours is temporal. Nothing in this life lasts, but our souls live on for eternity. Most importantly, people need to hear about the Gospel and we need to be bold in our testimony. May we seek this eternal vision, for this is the one that really counts.

Application

Read: Hebrews 11:1-6

Pray: for the greater vision of seeing things as God sees them — from a spiritual and eternal perspective.

Reflect: Have you experienced a situation that turned out differently than you thought? Share God's love with someone today, so that they have a chance to know Him too.

Day 6 - <u>Beauty in Chaos</u>

To every thing there is a season, and a time to every purpose under the heaven: A time to be born, and a time to die; a time to plant, and a time to pluck up that which is planted; Ecclesiastes 3:1-2

In our yard at the beach, we have a perennial garden, a perennial flowerbed and lots of pots for colorful annuals. Every spring I look at dismay at all the weeds that start to fill the gardens and then I pull up my sleeves, put on my gardening gloves and start yanking them out. While our front yard is well manicured and treed with nothing wild growing there, our back yard around the trellis fences and wall dividing our property from the neighbours is another story. It is an eclectic mixture of lush green vines, clover, and even deciduous trees that attempt to grow to full height, among other unnamed foliage. I've always tried to pluck them out to have a clean look, one that reduces both fall and spring clean-up.

But one year something changed. I had come through a difficult year where my mother-in-law had passed away and we also had to put down our 15 year old cat. We had to have our three tall pine trees taken down, and due to financial setbacks, we had to park our second vehicle that needed expensive repairs. It seemed that in every area, we were being tested to the limit. That spring, which was slow in coming due to inclement weather, I looked at all the wild things growing (more than usual due to the rain), and realized that rather than make the back yard look unkempt, it actually added to the ambience of it. The beginning of trees was generously covering a wall that needed to be painted. Vines were beginning to grow around the tree that's close to our shed. The tree itself that had begun as a twig provided shelter for the little mother wren that had a bird house with chicks close by. The new clematis plants were surrounded by other wild green plants, so pretty, I didn't

Day 6

have the heart to pull them out. So I decided for the first time to let the back yard unfold its own beauty since everything that was growing beyond my control seemed to have a purpose.

Many times in life, I have wanted my life to be perfect, ordered, and planned. But the year I had just come through had presented many events and situations I had no control over. Yet, somehow in the messiness of my life, God makes something beautiful out of it. He provided a beautiful condo for us in the city so my husband has a short drive to work each day. We don't have to worry about driving on winter roads or being stuck in a storm due to bad weather. He gave us two beautiful black cats that have a nice temperament and that we love. He's given us new friends. He even provided an honest, professional mechanic who fixed the van for us at a price we could afford, so we could take our camper out and enjoy summer days camping. He continues to surprise us with bouquets of love and joy in spite of ongoing difficulties. We look forward to seeing what He unfolds next.

King Solomon recognized something about time — that all events are really in God's hands and His timing is always perfect. May we learn to "go with the flow" and trust God as He unfolds His beauty in the midst of our trials and troubles.

Application

Read: Ecclesiastes 3:1-11

Pray: for appreciation of your circumstances and the faith to believe God is making something beautiful out of your life.

Reflect: Think of a time something beautiful came out of something difficult in your life. Write about it.

Day 7 - <u>The Discipline of Self</u>

Knowing that a man is not justified by the works of the law, but by the faith of Jesus Christ, even we have believed in Jesus Christ, that we might be justified by the faith of Christ, and not by the works of the law: for by the works of the law shall no flesh be justified. Galatians 2:16

    I once heard a guest on a Christian talk show talk about good works and how people sometimes use their own good works to gage how good they are as Christians. If they are not doing a lot of good works for others or are always aware of their short-comings, they fall into a sense of guilt and condemnation. If they feel they are always doing good works, then they become proud in their own accomplishments. In both instances, self, or the flesh (old man, sinful nature) is involved, which really means that since the focus is on self, God will not be getting the glory. Rather than it being "good works," it is actually "dead works," because it is not the work of the Holy Spirit. When it is the work of the Holy Spirit, we are no longer conscious of our own involvement in it, but are conscious of the Lord at work. When He is at work, He receives all of the glory.

    Being very interested in this subject, I took some notes when he said that a person becomes conscious of what they do, rather than being conscious of what God is doing. He also said that the works we do in the flesh are nothing more than dead works that we become slaves to doing. When I was looking up the above passage (Galatians 2:16), I looked up the word "justified." Another word for it is "free." Something happens when we give up our own idea of righteousness in trying to please God. We are freed from the treadmill of our own good works (dead works) and God starts doing His miraculous works, which give Him the glory.

    While listening to the show, I immediately thought about

Day 7

worry and fretting over upsetting situations and how this makes a person conscious of self. Also negative thinking and negative emotions are all-consuming. This is when the flesh is in full control instead of God. We may think we have things in hand, but fear actually controls us and robs us of a sound mind. So how do we overcome self? The Bible has much to say about this, but in my own experience when I am overly worried about a situation, such as going to the dentist or public speaking, I try very hard to re-focus my thoughts on what God's Word says. Sometimes I verbally quote Scripture that oppose fear, and sometimes I sing edifying and uplifting songs. Many times I have noticed a difference in my thought patterns and emotions. Also, I discover that the situation I was worried about was really nothing to worry about at all — I had simply allowed fear to dictate rather than let go and believe that God would take care of me.

Just as we take care of our body — we feed it, exercise it, wash it and so on, we also need to discipline our mind and emotions to line up with Scripture, and make sure our works are "His works," so our focus is on God and not on ourselves. It may take many times to do this and it is something we will need to practice daily. Even when we don't feel like it, we must not give up and fall back into our old ways where we allow "self" to control. When we do our small part, God will do His big part. May we be encouraged to know that God and His Word will never fail us.

Application

Read: Galatians 2:16-20

Pray: for God to reveal any areas of dead works in your life. Ask Him to help you re-focus on the works He does in your life.

Reflect: What areas do you need to give over to God so that He receives the praise? Be specific and then give them over to God.

Day 8 - <u>Our Father's Business</u>

And he said unto them, How is it that ye sought me? wist ye not that I must be about my Father's business? Luke 2:49

The first winter we moved out of the city to a resort town, we had blizzard after blizzard starting in November. Travel was difficult and perilous since there was often large snow drifts on the highway. We had just come home from the city where we had looked at a house to rent for what we believed would be a long and difficult winter. We had enjoyed supper at my sister's who lived nearby the rental house, then we headed towards home. What should have taken us one hour took us three hours due to the condition of the highways. When we arrived home, there were two messages on our answering machine — one from my sister and the other from my brother telling us that my mother was in the hospital.

This is not the kind of news you ever want to hear, especially when you live almost 200 miles away and it is blizzard conditions outside. I called my mom in the hospital right away and we prayed for her over the phone. Earlier that fall, I had started writing little tracts filled with encouragement and Scripture, and then printing them off at home. I was giving them to my family and friends to hand out, hoping to spread the good news of the Gospel wherever possible. Even though my mom was in semi-serious condition with a heart problem, she was so excited and shared that when she was able to get up and walk around, she went from room to room handing out these little tracts to other patients. She even left some in the waiting room. When she was explaining all this, she said, "I've got to be about my Father's business." She wasn't long in the hospital and I believe it's because God honored her for the work she had done for Him while there. Her life is a testimony of doing her heavenly Father's business and I'm sure a book could be written to record it all.

Similarly, her older brother had to be in the hospital for a minor operation. When he woke up from the anesthetic, he got out of bed and started going from room to room sharing about Jesus and the love of God. This was more important to him than sitting in bed thinking about his own troubles. He too was quickly healed and soon left the hospital. While this seems unusual and extremely admirable and selfless, it should really be the norm for all of us. When Jesus was still a child, His parents came looking for Him. They found Him in the temple preaching the Word of God from the Old Testament sacred Scriptures. Although His mother mentioned that He had worried them, He remained stedfast insisting that His heavenly Father's business was more important than even family obligations and ties. Mary didn't understand it all, but I believe she honored Him anyway and realized much later in His life that their son was indeed the "Son of God."

Are we going about doing our Father's business and is it a priority in our lives? The Father depends on us, so we need to push aside all other business, and do His work first.

Application

<u>Read</u>: Luke 2:40-52

<u>Pray</u>: that you will seek to do the Father's business over and above your own on a consistent basis.

<u>Reflect</u>: What does it mean to you to go about doing your Father's business? What will you do today to fulfill His calling for your life?

Day 9 - <u>Faith in Motion</u>

Even so faith, if it hath not works, is dead, being alone. James 2:17

Have you ever thought about faith and what it means when someone says, "Have faith"? Or perhaps you have read the many accounts of it in the Bible, and still wonder how you can attain it? When we think with our natural minds, faith seems illusive, a spiritual pie-in-the-sky especially when our needs are great whether they have to do with finances, health or relationships. When we are in need, or even when we are hoping for our dreams to come true, faith can seem so far out of reach that we give up and accept our lot rather than discover what faith really is and how it works. We all live by faith, yet few people really understand how extremely important it is and that nothing will work without it.

When I looked up the word "faith," I found it mentioned in 229 verses in the New Testament alone using the King James version of the Bible. When you start reading the verses that mention faith, you begin to realize just how important it is to God that we believe in Him and His many promises in the Bible (read Hebrews 11:6). But one day, I had a new revelation about faith. My husband and I were driving around our resort town and noticed that people were walking, cycling, swimming, boating or working in their yard. Everyone seemed to be doing something. I said to my husband, "Everything in life is meant to move. Life is motion." We are not meant to sit still and stagnate or watch TV by the hour and vegetate. Vegetating is for vegetables, not for people. Then I thought about the effects of what happens when we do nothing or begin to live sedentary lives. People, even children, become obese and overweight from lack of movement, then other problems are inevitable like heart problems, diabetes and arthritis to name a few. Too little activity can lead to depression and we feel more tired

Day 9

than usual. I believe we are all meant to be active as much as possible.

Faith works the same way. Many times we pray and then get discouraged when we don't have an immediate answer. Our thinking becomes "wishful" thinking and then we become discontent. While it is true, sometimes we do have to wait until God's perfect timing, many times the fault lies with us. I have found that in most cases, especially when I have goals to achieve, that it is I who must take a first step. If I need money, I must actively search for a job. If I need a friend, I must make myself available and make time for people. If I am always tired, I must take care of my body, go to bed early, eat properly and exercise. If I am unhappy, I must pray and read the Bible and ask God to comfort me and help me.

In the opening verse, James is saying that if you truly believe, you must act on it. In order to become a born-again believer, you must do something — pray the sinner's prayer of salvation (see back of book), believe in your heart, then receive the free gift of salvation. The way faith works does not change after we are saved. It is a timeless and eternal principle — faith requires action on our part, even if it means just saying a prayer. Imagine what will happen when we put our faith in motion and act on what we believe! Try it today.

Application

<u>Read</u>: James 2:14-26

<u>Pray</u>: for anything in your life that is a concern to you. Ask for wisdom in how to put your faith in motion and then do it.

<u>Reflect</u>: What does faith in motion mean to you? Set a goal to put your faith in motion starting today.

Day 10 - <u>Free-Fall</u>

He that dwelleth in the secret place of the most High shall abide under the shadow of the Almighty.
Psalm 91:1

    One day in the summer, a friend who is also our neighbour at the beach where we have a cottage, invited us over to enjoy a visit around their campfire. Her and her husband were living and working on a south Caribbean Island and were getting their cottage at the beach ready to sell. She was telling me about this amazing experience she had jumping from a parachute from a plane that had soared 10,000 feet into the air. She explained that she didn't jump by herself, but a trained parachute jumper was strapped to her to guide her fall and also safely guide her to the ground. I later learned that this is called "tandem" skydiving and is one of the best ways to begin skydiving and also one of the safest. The guide is like the driver and the beginner skydiver is like a passenger. In this way, the guide takes all the responsibilities while the passenger is along for the ride. I also discovered that over 3 million people attempt skydiving each year and that about 300,000 try skydiving with "tandem" jumps. Even though the sport can be very dangerous especially for the average person with little training, it is somehow comforting to know there is a trained guide who knows what to do in an emergency if one comes up.

    For my friend's jump, a photographer had recorded the entire experience, from the time she got on the plane to the time she jumped and then recorded the entire free fall to the ground. When she showed me the video on her laptop, I noticed the strangest thing. The guide covered my friend and they were both falling horizontally with their arms spread out like wings on a bird flying through the air. This position guided their flight to the ground.

    As I thought about this image, another image came to my

Day 10

mind. Many times in my life when I am going through a difficult situation and have felt alone and afraid, I have felt like I was falling out of an airplane with no one there to guide me to safety. Like air currants that can catch you up and whisk you away if you're skydiving and unprepared, sometimes life can be just as unpredictable. We may get hit with financial troubles, relationship problems, psychological or health ills, or any other number of things. Each time we may feel ill-prepared to deal with it. Yet, according to the opening Scripture, the Lord is constantly there to protect and guide us. He stretches out His wide wings and covers us from whatever life may throw at us. I have learned that He wants to take the responsibility and carry the weight of all my cares.

Read over that last part again. Why would God want to do this for me? A careful reading of Scripture will reveal that God loves us so much He longs to have a close personal relationship with us. Because He loves us, when things get really rough and hard to bear, He wants to take the greater burdens of our lives, and He wants us to be the passenger along for the ride. If you think of it, all of life is a free-fall because we don't know quite what to expect from one day to the next. But God does and all we have to do is allow Him to be our constant guide and companion.

Application

<u>Read</u>: Psalm 91

<u>Pray</u>: **Ask God to be your constant guide and companion in the good times and the bad.**

<u>Reflect</u>: **Have you ever felt like you were free-falling with no one to guide you to safety? Write about it and also past victories you have experienced. Share it with someone in need today.**

Day 11 - <u>Lowly in Heart</u>

Take my yoke upon you, and learn of me; for I am meek and lowly in heart: and ye shall find rest unto your souls. Matthew 11:29

One day during my devotional time I was reading the above passage of Scripture and felt that I should read it over more than once. I had read it over many times through the years and always thought that it meant I should take my burdens to the Lord through prayer when things were too difficult for me to bear. I also believe it meant that He is willing to take my burdens freely with no strings attached and no further obligation to Him on my part. That in itself has always meant so much to me — to think that God would care for me that much that He would be willing to take a huge cumbersome load off my shoulders and bear it for me! But this one day when I was really reading it, I realized that I didn't fully understand what He meant when He said He is, "meek and lowly in heart." I don't know or remember if a minister or pastor has ever elaborated on this particular Scripture in a way that made sense to me. So I asked the Lord what it meant.

Immediately I received an answer — "lowly in heart" has to do with pride, or the lack of pride in a person's heart. As soon as we are proud of something, we have just set a standard for ourselves that we must meet and usually this comes at a great cost. If I am a gardener and take great pride in my gardens, whether they are flower gardens, perennial gardens or vegetable gardens, then I must insure that they are watered, healthy, and weed-free. If I let them go and fail to take care of them, then I might worry that I will no longer hear the praises and "oohs" and "ahhs" of others at the great gardens I have created and maintained. Or if I have bought a new sports car, I want to keep it looking nice and polished, make sure it is regularly maintained and that the chrome on the wheels are sparkling.

Day 11

If I have lost weight and everyone says how much better I look, then I must continue to maintain my new weight. This is not to say any of these things are wrong to maintain, but if we take too much pride in something at the expense of neglecting our family, our prayer life and other good works for the sake of the Gospel, then perhaps we are overly concerned with the wrong things. To be sure, this kind of pride will keep us heavily burdened whether it be financial debt, over-tiredness or inadvertently creating envy and jealousy amongst friends. Humility always opens the door to true success in life, not self-centered pride.

Jesus was lowly in heart in the sense that everything He did was for the purpose of glorifying His heavenly Father. There was no pride in Him where the glory went to Himself. Isn't this an interesting concept? The labour that makes us weary and heavy laden is the work that we do where God is not glorified. This can be anything where we put "self" first. Jesus invites us to "learn of me" and then says "for I am meek and lowly in heart." This means that we don't just skim over these verses as I used to do, but stop and learn a lesson or two from the Great Teacher Himself. He may show you something else or something more that He didn't show me that will apply personally and be specific to you. I invite you to spend time with Him today.

Application

<u>Read</u>: Matthew 11:28-30

<u>Pray</u>: Give your burdens to the Lord today and spend time learning of Him.

<u>Reflect</u>: After you've spent time with the Lord, write out what He is teaching you and then share it with someone who needs an encouraging word today.

Day 12 - <u>Ease or Unease?</u>

And this is the condemnation, that light is come into the world, and men loved darkness rather than light, because their deeds were evil. For every one that doeth evil hateth the light, neither cometh to the light, lest his deeds should be reproved.
John 3:19-20

I once read an article in the newspaper about whether or not people felt uncomfortable or uneasy around evangelical Christians. The writer said that a recent poll stated that 31% of people feel uneasy around "born again" Christians. Although the article didn't state exactly why, it certainly made me and my husband pause for thought and take notice. We both agreed that 31% was a pretty low percentage and this must mean that we, as Christians are doing something wrong. We thought that maybe a lot more people should feel uneasy around us since, according to the above verses, they do not want to be faced with their own sinful lives. Then we wondered if perhaps we are not doing and saying enough to stand up for what and Who we believe in.

Also, many verses in the Bible say that we will be persecuted for our faith in some form or another. One is found in 2 Timothy 3:12: Yea, and all that will live godly in Christ Jesus shall suffer persecution. Yet, who would willingly volunteer to suffer and be persecuted because of his or her faith? In fact, it's not even a subject we want to talk about. But we need to stand firm regardless of whether people feel uneasy around us or not.

One afternoon my mother and I were discussing a Christian friend whose daughter had gone to university and as a result of liberal doctrination, turned away from Christianity and is not at all interested in returning to the God of her childhood. We discussed what can happen when a person attends a secular university and especially if they have

Day 12

enrolled in any of the general arts courses. Many educators endorse secular humanism and their books are required reading. Humanism is really the glorification of man and at the heart of their philosophy, is a belief that people are sovereign and don't need God or anyone else to tell them how to live their lives. Humanists would not like the Bible because God is sovereign and we, His created ones, are subject to His authority, both in this life and in the next. Humanists want complete autonomy and follow their own religion, which might be to try to save the environment or protect endangered animal or plant species. Many humanists claim to be atheists.

Is it any wonder a person not strong in their stand for God and His Word, could easily be led astray to believe in man-made religion? And is it any wonder that non-Christians will feel uneasy around Bible-believing Christians? Everything we believe flies in the face of most people who would rather be master of their own life and destiny. Our call is to be humble, to serve and trust in the living God who holds the future of the living and the dead in the palm of His hand. Our greatest joy and victory in life is to follow the steps of our Lord and Savior Jesus Christ, no matter how difficult our journey. Should non-Christians feel uneasy around us? Unless their hearts are searching and they long to know the Savior, we should expect them to feel uneasy. May we strive to continue to stand for the Lord even if it makes others feel uneasy.

Application

Read: 1 Peter 4

Pray: Ask God to search your heart for any belief system that is not based on God's Word, and ask Him to remove it.

Reflect: Have you ever been persecuted for your faith? What happened? Think of ways you can share your faith with people in spite of possible persecution.

Day 13 - <u>Coincidence or Providence?</u>

Now thanks be unto God, which always causeth us to triumph in Christ, and maketh manifest the savour of his knowledge by us in every place.
2 Corinthians 2:14

My husband and I were driving through a nearby city and noticed a church sign with an inscription on it. It said, "Coincidence is when God chooses to remain anonymous." At first I thought that was kind of interesting and perhaps had a ring of truth to it. I think it means that nothing in life happens by luck, chance or by accident. God is behind the interesting events in life that come together seemingly without human intervention. Is it coincidence when you meet someone you know from home when you're in an airport 1,000 miles from home? Or is it a coincidence when there is only one parking spot left for you close to the door when it's raining or just before the store is closing?

But as I thought more about the little saying, I wondered, Does God choose to remain anonymous? Why would He want to remain anonymous? Then my mind began to search Scripture and I couldn't think of one verse to substantiate this part of the above saying. Rather, all the verses that came to mind were just the opposite. God does want to make Himself known. He never ceases to want to make Himself known. Why? Because we humans have such a hard time believing in a divine God we cannot see, touch, hear or understand. We seek to communicate with Him with our natural senses. But God, knowing this about us, went the extra mile and went so far as to physically appear on earth through the body of His Son Jesus Christ, even though He is a Spirit. Many Scriptures reveal that He wants us to know Him. Indeed all of the Bible points to this and reflects this. And I believe God wants us to know it's Him because He longs to have a personal and meaningful relationship with us. This is proved to me time and time again, especially when I

Day 13

make an effort to read His Word or pray. He reveals Himself and reveals knowledge and His wisdom that is specific to my needs and or requests. He helps me to write every single devotional in these books. He gives what I need when I ask. I can only love Him more and trust Him more than I did yesterday. God is all about relationships.

One of my favorite books of the Bible is found in Job. The most interesting part to me is when Job has a conversation with God when He speaks to Job out of a whirlwind (see Chapter 38-41). Some of the most poetic and revealing passages about God and His indescribable and magnificent ways are written here. God chooses to reveal intricate and unknowable details of Himself and His creation. When God is finished talking, Job can only be awestruck and say:

> *I know that thou canst do every thing, and that no thought can be withholden from thee. Who is he that hideth counsel without knowledge? therefore have I uttered that I understood not; things too wonderful for me, which I knew not. Job 42:2-3*

Does God want to remain anonymous? I don't believe so. For a God of great love and unimaginable detail is interested in every aspect of our lives. And nothing under His sun is a coincidence.

Application

Read: 2 Corinthians 2:14-17

Pray: Ask God to reveal Himself to you each day. Thank Him for each time He has provided for you in unexpected and creative ways.

Reflect: How has God revealed Himself to you? Search the above Scriptures and any others you find in the Bible and write them down. Share about Him with someone today.

Day 14 - <u>In the Moment</u>

Which of you by taking thought can add one cubit unto his stature? Matthew 6:27

A well known religious TV program was offering people a free night out to hear all about the Book of Revelation, the last book in the Bible. The night out was to hear all about the future and what lies in store for humanity. At first I was intrigued by the idea, but there seemed that there was something not quite right about the whole idea. Although it is good to read all of the Bible and it is important to be aware of coming events, I believe that placing a greater focus on the future rather than focusing on the many concern's of a single day, is not what the Lord ever intended. We read the Book of Revelation to know ultimately who wins the final war with Satan against God and His people, both Israel and His redeemed Gentiles. Yet, there are religions that focus almost solely on prophetic or future events, but meanwhile miss seeing the great faithfulness and love of God in their everyday activities. Then there are also seers, clairvoyants, spiritualists (non-Biblically based) who claim they can know the future of both individuals and prophetic world events. But these types of people, who participate in looking into the future outside of God's authority, are condemned in the Bible. More than likely, they are getting their information from the wrong source, which is from Satan himself. And Satan can hardly be trusted to know the future with any accuracy, other than the punishment of eternal hell that awaits him.

I once heard a theologian say that our time on this earth is a preparation for eternity — how well we get to know God and how faithful we are to complete the tasks He's given us. But how can we handle our small tasks well if we are always concerned about a future that is not yet given us? And to take the future for granted, according to Proverbs 27:1, is "boastful." Why is it boastful to try to determine the future

Day 14

or even to make future plans? I believe it all has to do with our faith. Because we don't know the future, we need to trust God and communicate with Him on a daily basis. My husband and I have prayed many times over the years, and certainly when it comes to our vacation plans, since many times we have been stranded in strange places when a vehicle has broken down. Our faith has been stretched many times through trying and unpredictable circumstances. I believe God only gives us one day at a time, because how many of us could handle any more than that? Besides, if we knew too much about the future, then we wouldn't have to trust God for it.

When we first moved back to the city after buying a condo, we subscribed to the newspaper. I discovered a growing concern about gang-related crimes, and then started worrying about our safety. When I prayed about it, the Lord assured me not to be afraid because He is in control. Also, rather than focus on these negative things, we need to be busy doing our Father's business on a daily basis. So the next time someone comes to you with information about future events, check the source, and then take it all to God in prayer and leave it there. Take the peace He alone offers, and then get busy doing the work He has called you to do.

Application

Read: Matthew 6:25-34; James 4:13-16

Pray: about today and ask God what He wants you to know and do. Pray about any concerns you have in your future.

Reflect: Has your future turned out the way you predicted? What are some tasks you need to complete today? Do so, and then leave tomorrow and the future in God's capable hands.

Day 15 - <u>Weight Loss by Prayer</u>

Wherefore seeing we also are compassed about with so great a cloud of witnesses, let us lay aside every weight, and the sin which doth so easily beset us, and let us run with patience the race that is set before us, Hebrews 12:1

A few years ago, I started writing and researching my family history in earnest. My father wasn't well and was having trouble remembering things, so even though I had received his life story many years earlier, I wanted to make sure I had all of the little interesting stories he might have missed. Because I was sitting most of the time and it was during the winter, I failed to get exercise and noticed, to my dismay, that over the course of a few months I had gained 20 pounds. I had gained weight in my teen years, and had tried every diet imaginable, even starving myself to try to shed the unwanted pounds. And all throughout my 20s and early 30s had tried to lose an annoying 5-10 pounds with some success off and on. But I was more active then, swimming, walking and riding my bike on a regular basis.

But the rapid 20 pound gain, added to extra weight I had previously gained while a student in university, put me well over what I should have been. I was now entering an area on the weight charts that was considered "at risk" for many health problems like high blood pressure, diabetes, arthritis and heart problems, to name a few. What I did notice is that I was always tired, my joints ached due to the extra pressure, my feet hurt and I had to buy special orthopedic shoes, bike riding was uncomfortable, and walking was a test in endurance since I tired so easily. I felt like a prisoner in my own body and didn't even know where to begin to shed the pounds. One day I prayed and asked God to help me lose the 20 pounds I had gained. A few months later, I noticed that my throat was so dry I had trouble swallowing. I couldn't eat things like chips, dry toast, cookies or even hamburgers and chicken. So I started to eat half of my usual amount of food, and then started substituting dry food for wet food, like salads, soups, juices, fruit and so on. Almost a year later, I stood on the scale and my weight had dropped a total of 42 pounds. God had heard and answered my prayer, only He more than doubled the weight that I asked help for. Now, I feel much better, I can walk longer distances without tiring out, ride my bike, swim, take long flights of stairs and sleep much better at night.

I love the opening verse because I imagine a race track with people in the bandstands, watching us and cheering us on to run a different kind of race. Like my weight loss that took a year, we don't have to be fast, but we need to be faithful to continue doing the work that God has called us to do. But some of us are carrying extra weight, like worrying about money, our jobs, our health and our loved ones. Some of us are carrying too many things that we need to let go of from striving for material wealth and security to grandiose dreams that God will not bless. Any extra weight will weigh us down and impede our progress in running the race the Lord has set before us. Notice that this race is not a singular event. We have each other to lean on, so we need to pray together and work together, that we all finish with top scores, no one competing against the other.

Application

<u>Read</u>: 1 Corinthians 9:24-27

<u>Pray</u>: Ask God to reveal any extra weights you are carrying and then give them over to Him.

<u>Reflect</u>: Imagine yourself on God's race track. What do you need to let go of? What will you do to make your race more successful? Begin to do so today.

Day 16 - <u>Walking Off The Job</u>

For which of you, intending to build a tower, sitteth not down first, and counteth the cost, whether he have sufficient to finish it? Luke 14:28

The history of Manitoba is marked with many memorably and even tragic events that shaped what it is today. The Winnipeg General Strike in 1919 is one of them. Workers felt they were unable to live on their low wages since the cost of living had risen so dramatically. Employers ignored the concerns of the workers and seemed to be profiting, yet refused to raise wages. As a result, on May 15, 1919, a total of 12,000 workers walked off the job and shut down the city. Today, many union workers in free countries strike, like railroad workers and post office workers. When a paid union employee feels he or she can no longer make a decent living on their current salary due to rising cost of living costs, a union will often strike if employee needs are not adequately met by management.

More recently, a building contractor was hired to fix a balcony on a condo that was at risk of falling apart. They dismantled the balcony and began to fix the wall that had water damage. But once they had done this, they realized the amount of extra work involved (more than just replacing the balcony), and so they demanded more wages which the condo corporation was not prepared to pay. So they walked off the job and left the condo suite without a balcony and the wall unfinished. So many things in life seem like too much work and not enough reward for our efforts. I used to not like cooking because I would spend hours preparing a meal only to have it eaten within 15-20 minutes. Then after the meal I'd have to spend another few hours in the kitchen cleaning up. It didn't take long for me to decide to learn how to cook quick meals in only 15-30 minutes that were just as good and required less baby-sitting. I could cook a delicious stew in the crock-pot and leave it. Or better yet, I could buy

Day 16

pre-cooked chicken, salads and fresh rolls and have nothing to do but carve the chicken and stick a spoon in each salad.

In the Bible, Jesus talks a lot about counting the cost if we are to be His followers. Many people were interested in the works that Jesus was doing because they had never witnessed such miracles. Crowds would follow Him to see what miracle He would perform next. But Jesus never came to the earth to entertain people, but to minister to their needs. Throughout His ministry many accounts are given where Jesus tests the true heart and intention of those who are following Him. He wanted followers who would be faithful and also share the same mission He had. There was never any room for entertainment or fickle followers, who, once they tired of His path, would turn away and go on to the next latest fad. In John 6, Jesus reveals His deity and the future cross He must bear. Many followers turn away not wanting to hear the high cost of being His follower. Like the workers in the Winnipeg General Strike, they felt the commitment was too high for the reward, so walked away. Yet, they also could never experience the numerous joys that Jesus gives, not the least enjoying a close relationship with Him and future eternal rewards. May we be His faithful ones, true to His call, no matter how high the cost.

Application

Read: John 6:47-66

Pray: for strength and a faithful heart to follow Jesus when the going gets rough. Ask Him to be your constant Friend and Guide.

Reflect: Have you ever walked away from a difficult job? Why and what happened? List the costs and rewards of being a follower of Jesus. Share your faith today.

Day 17 - <u>Does God Care?</u>

Bless the LORD, O my soul, and forget not all his benefits: Psalm 103:2

Every once in awhile I believe things happen to turn our attention towards God. On a long weekend one summer, many things seemed to go wrong. Friday evening I was driving in a nearby town and was chewing a piece of gum when one of my expensive crowns came off with the gum. Everything would be closed until Tuesday and this is not good to leave a tooth exposed for that long. I always carry a phone book in the vehicle, so I quickly looked for a dentist who takes emergency cases. There was only one office open the next day and it was in the city more than an hour away. I might not be able to get in. I called my husband who happened to be at home and asked him to give me my own dentist's home number. So I called and left him a message telling him what had happened.

In the meantime, I was greatly distressed and my mother was staying with me, so she prayed that the crown I had put back in its place would stay and that I would be able to get in to see a dentist as quickly as possible. My dentist called me a couple hours later and said he would fix my tooth the following morning in his office in the city even though his office is normally closed on Saturday. When I got to the dentist's the next morning, the crown had not only stayed in its place, but was even difficult to take out so he could glue it back in again! Truly God had answered our prayers!

The day before another strange thing happened! My mother and I were driving to a nearby town and every time a car passed us on the highway I could hear a strange "whoosh" sound, almost like a surround sound in the van. I had never heard such a strange sound when a car was passing by. I checked the air conditioner, then my mother said that maybe it was my ears, since I had an ear infection and

Day 17

couldn't hear properly out of my left ear. Then she said she could hear the strange "whoosh" sound too. I hoped there was nothing wrong with the van since it had already cost us plenty to fix it only weeks before. I thought I'd look for any open windows, then I spotted something unusual through the rear-view window on the passenger side. The back window was open! I had left it open to take out some things we had bought before we drove on to Gimli. So we were driving with the hatch open in the back which caused the strange "whoosh" sound and had also made my rear-view much clearer! God had protected us yet again!

Saturday night, both lenses fell out of my mother's prescription glasses, and she couldn't see without them. My husband found that one of the tiny screws was missing. We had just moved and trying to find the little screw driver and glasses kit was a challenge. But I found the screw driver and he found the kit. Soon we had fixed her glasses and she could wear them and see again! Truly God is good! He had helped us and protected us in every trying circumstance. My mother believes in praying over everything, no matter how small or insignificant. Does God care and answer prayer? We believe He does and He's interested in every detail of our lives. Pray and trust Him today to do the same for you!

Application

Read: Psalm 103:1-11

Pray: every day for God to heal you, protect you and provide for you. Praise Him for all He will do and all He does for you.

Reflect: When are some trying times you have had where God has answered your prayers? List the many ways God cares for you. Share His goodness with someone today.

Day 18 - Helping Hands

They helped every one his neighbour; and every one said to his brother, Be of good courage.
Isaiah 41:6

My husband and I are members of a local farmers market that sets up tables every Saturday morning for the summer and part of the fall. We sell mainly hand-made jewelry, cards and books. The market is an overall success because each member is included in the decision-making process which occurs at an annual meeting held before the market starts. But even more important, each member takes care to help other members when needed. For instance, a member beside us makes beautiful quilts and wall-hangings. Every once in awhile I have not had time to sort out all my jewelry, and she sees the predicament I'm in and always offers to help sort out tangled necklaces and also find missing earrings if a strong wind blows my displays over.

Another time, a member had trouble setting up a tent cover, so my husband rushed over and helped set it up and even repair it when the ropes would not support the legs. The member was so pleased and grateful that she gave us a jar of home-made honey-apple jam. Other members have given us a discount, one on a big container of honey and another on two hand-made wooden foldable tables, simply because we are members. I asked if our tables could be set up on the sunny side of the area we are designated. A week later, another member had to quit, so the organizers immediately thought of us and gave us their spot on the sunny side. Other times, we help each other load and unload our goods when needed. Thoughtfulness and generosity abounds and I am so proud to be a member of such a group!

I realized that there are definite privileges and benefits to belonging to a group especially one we are committed to! This reminds me also that as a Christian, the benefits and

Day 18

privileges are so numerous and rewarding that they couldn't be all written down here. God has done and does everything for us, from saving us from a godless eternity, to rewarding us daily with all His many blessings. But when we are willing to help others, there are even greater benefits that He showers on us. If you think of it, most things in this life are accomplished by a group effort. A church would not exist as we know it if there was just a pastor and no congregation. A choir needs more than one person to bring out all the various tones and sounds that blend together to make it sound worshipful and inspiring.

In the opening verse, they not only helped each other, but encouraged each other as well. When we are alone too much without human interaction and fellowship, it is easy to become discouraged. Our tasks might take longer to complete and we might feel like giving up. Sometimes all we need to do is talk to one other person to feel encouraged. But belonging to a group with a shared cause, and participating in it, is even a greater form of fellowship and can yield many positive benefits. This is what the farmers market has demonstrated to me, and this is what it is really all about, especially as Christians part of a world-wide Body of Christ. May we take every opportunity to lend a helping hand wherever needed!

Application

Read: Acts 2:44-47

Pray: for God to show you where help is needed. Ask Him for a willing heart to selflessly give to others.

Reflect: Have you ever been part of a group that helps and supports each other? Write about it. Find someone you can help today and make yourself available to them.

Day 19 - <u>Sounds in the Night</u>

Behold, he that keepeth Israel shall neither slumber nor sleep. The LORD is thy keeper: the LORD is thy shade upon thy right hand. Psalm 121:4-5

Everyone has different sleep patterns. Some people do strange things while they sleep like sleep-walk or talk. Still others snore so loudly they wake everyone up in the house. There are also sleep disorders that prevent people from having a good night's sleep, like insomnia, which is at the top of the list for the most common sleep disorder. There is also sleep apnea, when a person stops breathing temporarily while sleeping, and there is also narcolepsy, when a person cat naps during the day without planning to. Many people, with or without known sleep disorders, wake up tired and never seem to get a good night's sleep.

For me, I need a fairly dark room and quietness, although I don't mind the sound of a fan or a distant train. But some people can sleep anywhere like on a plane, train, bus, or in the passenger seat of a moving vehicle. However well we sleep and whatever the conditions, I am sure everyone can relate to being unexpectedly woken up. One night, such a thing happened to me and my two kittens. A few days earlier, we had bought a floor model upright air conditioner that has two hoses you attach to a bar and then sandwich it between an open window and the window frame. We needed it in our third floor bedroom since it was turning out to be a hot summer. But one night it was very cool outside and I needed to take the hoses out of the window frame, close the window and wheel the air conditioner out of the way. I climbed into bed, had fallen asleep after awhile and all of a sudden, I heard a strange unidentifiable sound that startled me and my kittens. Both my kittens stood straight up and then jumped to the floor. I could see them both very cautiously approaching the wall where the window is.

Day 19

The wide hoses on the air conditioner were bent awkwardly and hanging sideways. They had partially slid down the wall, causing the strange noise that had woken us up. So with that, I went back to bed. Meanwhile, the kittens had settled themselves on the edge of my bed side-by-side tensely watching for more action from the "monster" hoses. Sure enough, every few seconds, the hoses continued to slide intermittently down the wall making the strangest noise. Every time they slid, the kitties would jump, jolting me out of my sleep. Finally, my husband got up and put the hoses away properly which ended the action "show" for our kittens.

Through the years, I have woken up many times from nightmares, loud noises, or have had trouble sleeping from worrying about too many concerns of the day. I have often found great comfort in reading the opening verses, knowing that there is nothing to fear and that a good sleep (or returning to sleep after being unexpectedly woken up) can really be as simple as a prayer. If we turn everything over to God, then truly He becomes our "keeper," handling all the many affairs that cause us worry or concern. Many times, when I have been unable to sleep, I have prayed mostly for others until I fall asleep and my sleep is that much sweeter because the Lord rewards me with peace. The next time you can't sleep, try prayer — this works better than a sleeping pill any day.

Application

Read: Psalm 121

Pray: Ask God to be your Keeper day and night and when you can't sleep remember to pray for others.

Reflect: Recall times when you've been unable to sleep. What did you do to finally fall asleep? How has God been your Keeper and what will you do to ensure your sleep is good and peaceful?

Day 20 - <u>After Retirement?</u>

Trust in the LORD with all thine heart; and lean not unto thine own understanding. In all thy ways acknowledge him, and he shall direct thy paths.
Proverbs 3:5-6

 One day me and a friend, who has been retired for a couple of years already, discussed the pros and cons of retirement. He said that one of the things that was the most difficult to adjust to was the lack of routine. When we work we are on a set schedule — we get up at a certain time, have our breakfast, drive or catch the same bus to work each day, have similar duties to perform and most often, work with the same people. In this sense, our life seems more safe and predictable, and our thoughts are more focused since things are pretty much laid out for us. There can be great comfort in living in the familiar, with few unexpected demands on us.

 Retirement, on the other hand, presents new challenges. Our schedule disappears, which at first, seems like a tremendous freedom, since now we can sleep in and go to bed late. We can attend to all of the things we put aside when we were chained to a work schedule. We might be able to go to late night movies, or spend time pursuing a favorite hobby or sport, or visit friends and family more often. But after awhile, especially if our spouse is still working, wisely managing our time can seem almost insurmountable, especially if we haven't carefully planned for our retirement. And it's not just retired people that struggle with this. People who are suddenly laid off and are without employment, or people who are ill for extended periods of time may also struggle with time management. Even people in certain jobs, like sales, or work-at-home businesses and are expected to work independently, may struggle with time management. Too much time to manage can be a detriment to productivity just as too little time can be.

Day 20

In writing these books, I must push aside many things in order to complete my daily writing goals. This takes discipline and a constant reminder to myself that writing and completing the books are more important than laundry, housework, shopping and even talking to friends on the phone. For someone who doesn't have a worthy goal, managing time will seem a waste of time because there isn't a strong enough motivation and purpose behind the activity they are doing. Many books are written about time management and how to best use time to complete and exceed given tasks. There are even some pretty good books out there to give us new ideas on how to dream and pursue our dreams. I've read many of them myself. But since I have been retired from the normal day to day work life outside of the home, I have learned many things about time management from the Bible, and God continues to show me more. First, He has taught me to put Him first by praying and reading His Word. This puts my thoughts in order. Second, I am to be quiet and listen for the Lord's instruction for the day. Third, I am to do what the Lord instructs and trust Him unswervingly that what He directs is His very best for me for that day. Fourthly, there are times I need to be quiet and not have any schedule at all. I have learned not to be afraid of the quietness, but accept it and see where it leads me. Doing the above has yielded a fruitful life for me and I know it will also work for you.

Application

Read: Proverbs 3:1-18

Pray: Seek God first thing every day. Listen for His instruction, then ask Him to help you do what He says to do.

Reflect: Do you struggle with time management? What will you do to better manage your time? Write down your goals and work out a plan. Share it with someone and ask them to help keep you accountable. Offer to do the same for them.

Day 21 - <u>The Wrong Fit</u>

When I was a child, I spake as a child, I understood as a child, I thought as a child: but when I became a man, I put away childish things.
1 Corinthians 13:11

When I was just a little girl of about five years old, I put my dad's big shoes on, placed his too-big hat on my head and picked up his large briefcase. This was the look of a traveling salesman and I wanted to be just like him. A close neighbour friend of the family came over, saw me, laughed and said, "She's a little Dave." David was my father's name. Often, children imitate their parents or another adult and play dress-up. It's fun when you're a kid trying to act grown-up. It's cute to see kids wearing all the wrong sizes and colors, but still, if it doesn't fit, the outfit eventually becomes cumbersome and awkward to walk around in. Little girls might try to wear their mother's high heels and soon they fall flat on their face. A little boy might try on his dad's hip-waders he uses for hunting or fishing, and also find them so cumbersome he soon wants out of them.

In the same way, once we grow up, it doesn't take long to realize that sometimes our lofty dreams are too big for our size and no matter how hard we try, our dreams don't fit our paycheck. For me, I had always wanted to be a successful writer, whether this meant being the magazine editor of a prestigious woman's magazine, or writing best-selling romance fiction novels. Yet, no matter how hard I tried to secure gainful employment to lead me in this direction, the doors were never fully opened for my dreams to become a reality. I also wanted to own my own expensive house close to or on a lake. I wanted to travel the world over. I soon discovered that the position of writing could never begin to pay for such lofty and expensive things. So I would apply for other jobs, like management jobs that paid well. But of course, I wasn't qualified, so I wouldn't even get an

Day 21

interview. Then when I started writing and publishing devotional books, I thought a publisher would buy them and print off hundreds to thousands of copies, distribute them and I would simply collect the royalties. But this hasn't happened.

Also, I heard of a friend in a similar situation. Also a writer, she hopes to gain notoriety and that bigger companies will notice her and she will become well-known. As I thought about her situation and mine, I realized that in some ways I had returned to my childhood, trying on clothes that are too big to fit me, and that, more importantly, my dreams do not fit God's plans for my life. While I wholeheartedly believe that God gives us dreams, and also opens the door to our every success, I believe that there are two things far more important to Him than our big lofty dreams. The first is, that our hearts are wholeheartedly devoted to Him, and secondly, that our dreams do not become more important than the day-to-day duties He has assigned us. In other words, that we are faithful to Him no matter what the outcome. So if your dreams haven't materialized, it doesn't mean that they won't. It simply means that either the time isn't right, or that maybe your dreams are the wrong fit for you, and for what God has in mind for you. May we always remain faithful to Him and trust Him to give us dreams that fit.

Application

Read: 1 Corinthians 2:1-12

Pray: Ask God for wisdom regarding your dreams. Ask Him to reveal His dreams for you.

Reflect: What are your greatest dreams? Do you feel they fit you and that you and God can fulfil them? What will you do towards fulfilling them?

Day 22 – <u>Righting Wrongs</u>

Therefore thou art inexcusable, O man, whosoever thou art that judgest: for wherein thou judgest another, thou condemnest thyself; for thou that judgest doest the same things. Romans 2:1

One of the easiest things to do when we see an injustice is to immediately want to condemn it and wish that person speedy retribution. Sometimes we ourselves put on robes of a judge and try to right a wrong, but this is rarely successful. For instance, if someone cuts us off in traffic, we might immediately respond by honking the horn and then feel justified that we have evened the score, but this hardly rights a wrong. It only aggravates the situation. How easy it is to spot another's weakness and ignore our own.

One of the most viable areas where we see people judging each other is in the church itself. One denomination may think they are superior to another, whether all are of the Christian faith or not. Rarely do you see different denominations worshiping together. People within the same church separate from each other due to hurts and indifferences. Cliques are common where some are accepted and embraced and others are on the outside, shunned and left out. Such cliques cause so much pain and division that they are destined to fail. A church cannot prosper and be blessed when members of Christ's Body suffer at the hands of other members. In fact, I know of two churches where such cliques prevailed, but both churches have since undergone a complete turnover in members and those cliques no longer exist.

Judgment is always and only ever in the realm of God's work, because He is just and knows all things. Can we say we are really qualified to determine what is right in the first place? Are we sure that our judgments are in the best interest of another, or are we just self serving our own sinful flesh? Jesus was emphatic in every reference to judging another — He outright condemned it.

Many years ago, I learned a lesson about judging another. A co-worker had said such cutting things to me, that I couldn't find room in my heart to forgive her. The Lord showed me that when He died on the cross, He already forgave her for that sin against me. Then He showed me how I was keeping her from her rightful freedom in Christ by not forgiving her, and also that no freedom or healing was possible until I agreed to forgive her and forget the incident. Truly the opening verse took on a personal meaning for me. As long as I condemned her, I was also condemning myself. The only way to make things right was to forgive her. When I did so, I was set free and had no more hard feelings towards her; and, I was able to enjoy working with her again.

When we judge others, we cut ourselves off from giving God free reign in our hearts to love people. We do more harm to ourselves than anyone else. When we judge, we ourselves will also be judged. If there is someone you have a hard time forgiving, set them free by being willing to forgive them. Watch what God will do to restore your peace of mind and, if possible, your relationship with that person.

Application

Read: Romans 2:1-13

Pray: Ask God to reveal your heart and show you any areas of unforgiveness. Make things right with God and others.

Reflect: How do you handle injustice? What are some benefits of allowing God to right wrongs instead of you? Make things right with someone you feel has unjustly wronged you.

Day 23 - <u>An Aging Population</u>

But lay up for yourselves treasures in heaven, where neither moth nor rust doth corrupt, and where thieves do not break through nor steal: For where your treasure is, there will your heart be also. Matthew 6:20-21

Recently, I read that the world's population is aging rapidly. This means that there are more elderly people than younger people. The article suggested that there is an overall reduction in fertility rates even in developing countries. And in developed countries, like those in North America and most of Europe, one in every five people are over the age of 60.

So what does this mean for the world in general? It means that there are fewer people working to support various old age pensions and fewer consumers since there is a marked drop in spending once a person reaches the later stages of life, assuming their needs have changed and they already have bought all they really need. It also means fewer people will pay income tax and property tax since people are retired and many sell their homes to live in an apartment or seniors home. This really changes the whole structure of social programs in countries like Canada who depend on a working population to support various social programs like Medicare plus a number of other social programs that depend on the generous tax contributions that are imposed on the working class. As part of the solution, already, in many professions, the age of retirement has been pushed from 65 to 70 and even older than that. Teachers, for example, do not have a specific retirement age. They can teach well into their senior years without mandatory retirement and some do.

But, for many people, by the time they reach 60 or 65 they are tired and burned out from their many years of working, which might add up to 40 years or more already. So the prospect of retiring without some kind of pension to pay one's necessary bills is a frightening one indeed, especially if a person is unable to continue to work and is counting on a pension as the only means of support.

Yet, at any stage of a person's lifetime, a job can end and so can a monthly paycheck. A person can get fired, or suddenly become ill and become unable to work. The real issue is, not so much, Where will my next meal come from and how will I pay my rent or mortgage? But it is, How much have I invested in the Kingdom of God, in terms of what is really important? Have I given Him what is most valuable to me, such as time and tithe and have I done it wholeheartedly with all I am and have? Every time I give to God, I am really investing for my future, not only in heaven, but also during my time here on earth. I have seen God miraculously provide for me when I was unable to work and had no job or any prospect of money coming in. I have seen Him do the same for others. He never fails to provide and He never goes back on His Word. So I believe our focus need not be the concerns of our future retirement and whether we have stored enough money in the bank to be comfortable. Rather, our constant focus needs to be on how much we are contributing to the Kingdom of God. For when we trust Him with our investments, we have a sure provision and reward no matter how rapidly the world is aging and changing.

Application

Read: Matthew 6:19-34

Pray: for God to show you where He wants you to invest in His Kingdom.

Reflect: What are your thoughts on your own retirement? How can you best invest in the Kingdom of God? Do so today.

Day 24 - <u>True Freedom</u>

Stand fast therefore in the liberty wherewith Christ hath made us free, and be not entangled again with the yoke of bondage. Galatians 5:1

It is well known that some countries who have lived for many years under strict dictatorships and then been given freedom from their tyrannical rulers, soon struggle with their new independence and some even want the dictatorship back in power. This sounds bizarre and yet we can understand it if it is the only life they have ever known. To be given freedom can be a frightening prospect because now there are fewer boundaries and the security of having one's decisions made is gone. In short, there are many responsibilities that go with a person's freedom.

One well-known writer stayed in an institution for the mentally ill so that he could experience life as a patient in order to do real and legitimate research for a book he was writing. Astoundingly, he later reported that after about two weeks, he didn't want to leave the institution. He became used to being waited on and he found security in the daily routines that were laid out for him. All he had to do was obey whatever orders he was given. Other organized institutions, like correctional ones, offer inmates three square meals a day, enforced work and other duties that go with serving their time. Some inmates, when they are released from their prison term, find the transition into normal life too difficult. Some can't get jobs and others have no place to go but the hell they left behind, so they deliberately break their parole, so that they can return to the safety and predictability of the institution.

Then there are patients in hospitals who find the same kind of security when they must stay for an extended period of time. Somehow it is comforting to have your meals specially made and a doctor and nurses attending to your

Day 24

every concern. Rarely does real life provide this once we've grown up and left home and are on our own. There are communes and ethnic groups where groups of families live and work together. They share household duties, schooling, workloads and expenses for the benefit of all. It would be easy to get used to this kind of communal living and you would think that a person would rarely ever feel lonely or overwhelmed by the many demands of life.

Similarly, in our spiritual lives, Jesus Christ offers us a freedom from our old sinful life, freedom from living for ourselves and freedom and permission to access His presence and His throne, not to mention freedom to enter His heaven where we will spend eternity with Him. It is a freedom unsurpassed that we can experience simply by believing in Him and accepting Him into our hearts and lives. Yet, many people turn back and return to their old sinful life. Like any other freedom, we must also fight for this one and maintain our freedom in Christ and also walk in this newness of life that He's so graciously provided. To turn back may be easy to do and we may be tempted to live a life of slavery to the flesh, but this is a life that yields no beneficial fruits in our lives. May we continue to work at living in this freedom and then enjoy all the perks of what Christ has already done for us.

Application

Read: Romans 6:6-23

Pray: Ask God to give you a new freedom in your walk with Him. Ask for help in continuing to walk in the freedom He's provided.

Reflect: What is your definition of freedom? How do you handle your freedom? Share God's love with someone who needs a new freedom in their life.

Day 25 - <u>Reliable Sources</u>

Knowing this first, that no prophecy of the scripture is of any private interpretation. For the prophecy came not in old time by the will of man: but holy men of God spake as they were moved by the Holy Ghost. 2 Peter 1:20-21

Today is known as the information age probably more than at any other time in history. People are hungry for information. There are many sources where we can get information — the daily newspaper, various websites, television news stations, the radio, even our next-door neighbours.

It is well known that general public media sources such as newspapers are fed by advertising dollars, and therefore must in some ways, be sensitive to their advertisers preferences. In journalism terms, it's called, slanted news, and may even show preference to certain religions and political persuasions and even shun others. In one of my city newspapers, for instance, Christianity has been made fun of or mentioned in almost strictly negative and sarcastic ways. So then I begin to wonder how many other articles are slanted and do not have legitimate research backing them? Are they simply opinion pieces to grab people's attention? Or are they worth their weight in journalistic integrity, accuracy, and backed by careful research?

If I were a student writing a serious college essay, for example, I would never use the newspaper as a reliable source. And as a teacher, when I have the opportunity to give students assignments to write essays, I insist that they use a variety of sources that are reliable and ones that they must document. Books and journal articles are usually well researched and are a much better source for accurate information, but they are not always right with their information either. Even when articles are well researched,

Day 25

I still want to know something about the author, their background and position on key issues, especially if it is a book that has to do with the Christian faith.

When I first started writing a book about backsliding, I wanted to research it as thoroughly as possible. So I started buying as many books as I could find that related to backsliding. After reading many books that gave me ideas and contributed to some of my thoughts (especially the commentaries on Jeremiah), I wrote the first draft, using many of my sources, and ended up with a polished manuscript. But this is not what God had in mind for me. He wanted me to write another version of it and use only the Bible as my ultimate source. So I did that and learned so much more from personal revelation than from someone else's experience. The Bible, I discovered, is the most reliable source there is, not just in dealing with issues of our faith, but in every issue in life. It has answers for every kind of relationship, every kind of science including meteorology and the cosmos, medical issues, future events, carpentry and building and much much more. No other book explains the human heart as well as this one does. It is an AMAZING LIFE-CHANGING book unsurpassed by any other. And it is completely 100% accurate in all it's detail. The Bible is the best authority for all matters in life, for it is as reliable as God Himself, a "sure foundation." May we take every advantage to read it, study it and consider it the most reliable source of all.

Application

Read: 2 Timothy 2:15-26

Pray: Ask God to open up His Word to you when you read it, and pray for discernment in everything you read.

Reflect: What has the reading of the Bible done for you? What are some major things you have learned from it? Read at least two chapters a day from your Bible and take notes. Begin today.

Day 26 - <u>Earthen Vessels</u>

But we have this treasure in earthen vessels, that the excellency of the power may be of God, and not of us. 2 Corinthians 4:7

Recently, I heard the testimony of a well-known gospel singer who travels and sings with a world-renowned group of various gospel singers. He had come from a very painful and broken past. As a result he had struggled with his Christian faith even though he had been very successful as a Christian artist. Even with the support of other Christian friends who came along side him when he needed them, it still wasn't enough to provide the healing that he needed in his life. But something happened to change things around. He shared that through all his suffering and pain, Jesus came into his life in a way that was so real and so powerful that his pain was gone and his life was changed forever. In fact, as he shared this part of his testimony you could see the love and joy of God in his eyes and on his face. When he sang songs about Jesus, he was now singing from the very depths of his soul, because Jesus was real to him and had made such an indelible impact and noticeable difference in his life.

One of the things he shared was that although we are just earthen vessels, we hold inside of us this incredible treasure, the Lord Jesus Himself. After he shared, it brought to mind the idea of being an earthen vessel. If you have ever seen pottery being formed, you will know that it takes a great skill to form the clay into a perfect round vase or bowl and that the wheel must spin at just the right tempo. Then you have to fire the clay so that it hardens, and then hope that your piece is made well enough to stand the pressure of the ovens without cracking or caving in. When you have the finished piece, it will now be useful as a vase or water jug or whatever use you have in mind for it.

Overall, the purpose of an earthen vessel is to be able to

Day 26

use it. God wants to use us. So like in the case of the Christian singer, God uses our weaknesses for His purposes and sometimes this is the only way He can reach us. But when we are full of ourselves and our own righteousness, we need to be broken and remolded — to not only hold the King of Kings in our heart, but also to be used, that others see Him and not us. In my own life, I was once full of my own sinful desires and had no relationship with God at all. But everything in my life fell apart because I was involved in things I shouldn't be. God had to get my attention and He used my failures to do so. One of the most miraculous things He did for me was to change my desires, from wanting to live a sinful godless life to wanting to live for Him. He allowed me to experience the beauty of His holiness and the unearthly peace and rapturous joy of being in His presence. He reached out His loving Hand of friendship to me and He offered me free restitution. I grabbed on to Him never wanting to let go. Since then, my life has been marked with many joys and many sorrows, but I know one thing is for sure — nothing is greater than knowing He can use me as a vessel, to show his love, His power and His beauty. May we always be willing to be broken, that He can show His most excellent work through us.

Application

Read: 2 Corinthians 4:7-17

Pray: Ask God to use you as an earthen vessel. If you are going through difficulties, ask God to use them for His glory.

Reflect: How has God used your weakness for His glory? Write it down and then share it with someone who needs to be encouraged today.

Day 27 - <u>Passing a Test</u>

Moses said to the people, "Do not be afraid. God has come to test you, so that the fear of God will be with you to keep you from sinning." Exodus 20:20 NIV

The first time I can remember where I had to study for and pass a test was in grade school. Even in grade two I had to pass math tests and spelling tests in order to make it into the next grade. I never really looked forward to receiving my report card even though I did well throughout grade school. In high school the tests were even harder — I had to pass tests in Biology, English, French and Math and wondered many times if I would even make it to Grade 12. But I did. Then when I was 16, I wanted my drivers license, so I had to study to pass the written exam and also learn how to parallel park for the practical test.

After Grade 12, I entered college life and the tests and exams were even more challenging. But if I was to be a journalist, I had to make the grade. Then after one year of college, I went to Bible School and had to pass tests there as well. By the time I was 19, I felt as if I'd been in school all my life. But these were really some of the best years of my young life, studying and learning lessons that would aid me later on. After college, I worked in the clerical field for a few years. But after awhile I found that I was getting nowhere with little hope of getting promoted to jobs that really interested me. In my late 20s I made a decision that I really wanted to continue in the writing field and that I would work in the clerical field only to pay my bills so I could learn the craft of writing. So I started applying for good-paying jobs at each level of government, the City, the Province and the Federal Government. They all paid well and had excellent benefits. But there was one condition before any of these institutions would hire me — I had to pass a typing test and score 55 wpm or higher. Finally, I passed and was eventually hired full time with the Provincial

Day 27

Government. It paid my bills as I attended the university part-time for six years. I couldn't begin to count the exams I wrote in those six years. But if was worth it, because it paved the way for me to take another two years of university to become a certified teacher. Now, rather than take tests, I would be giving them. What a challenging job!

When I think about tests as a means to move forward and succeed in life, I think of another kind of test, the kind that God gives. Just as we need to pass tests throughout our life in order to move forward, God gives us tests as well, in order that we might grow and also to protect us. In the opening verse, Moses tells the children of Israel that God is going to test them in order to prevent them from sinning. What an interesting concept. God was going to be with them and reveal Himself in order to protect His people from destroying themselves. If they had a reverence for Him in their hearts, they would have no need to turn away from Him and sin against Him. It would all be done with the utmost care and love — God would never abandon them. What a priceless treasure, to know and serve a God who cares that much about us. Perhaps you have been going through tests of every kind in your life and you wonder why. Be assured, God knows the final outcome — all you have to do is trust. He'll make sure you pass with flying colors.

Application

<u>Read</u>: James 1:12-18

<u>Pray</u>: for God to help you if you are undergoing trials and tests. Pray for others who are also being tested.

<u>Reflect</u>: What are some difficult spiritual tests you have gone through? What was the outcome? Write about it.

Day 28 - <u>Sharing Good News</u>

And he said unto them, Go ye into all the world, and preach the gospel to every creature. Mark 16:15

Have you ever been so excited about something that you were just bursting to tell someone your good news? I can think of many times in my life when this has happened, like when I got hired at Via Rail through a series of circumstances that only God could have orchestrated. Also, when I got engaged to my husband we couldn't wait to break the news to our relatives, friends and co-workers. God had performed a miracle for us to enable us to get married. When we bought our first home, there was the joy and excitement of settling into a resort area with a beautiful lake just down the street. When we adopted our two cats, Latte and Espresso, we phoned everyone we knew. Even buying a new car or winning something unexpected is cause for excitement and celebration. Whenever I receive new kitchen products from the company I sell for, and then use them, I want to invite people over to show them how easy they are to use and how easily they can cook up delicious meals using these new kitchen tools.

But the greatest news of all that I couldn't wait to share was when Jesus had done a miraculous work in my heart and then changed my life. I wanted everyone to know and shared each time He revealed something new. It didn't matter to me what people thought. I was just so happy, I wanted to share the joy and I wanted people to know how great my God is and that He could do the same for them. He continues to change me and reveal His truths, many of which I share in these books. At first, most people listened and wanted to know what on earth could make someone so deliriously happy. Who doesn't want to hear good news when there seems to be so much negative news out there, and people are struggling just to get through the day?

Day 28

If you read the accounts of the disciples in the Gospels of the New Testament, and especially the Book of Acts, you discover the exuberance and the joy of the disciples and apostles who risked their own life for the sake of sharing the Gospel. Sharing our testimony isn't about doing good works and adding to our rewards in heaven. But it is about sharing an incredibly life-changing and exciting opportunity with others. We not only want to offer them Jesus and the new life He freely gives, but we want to offer them a chance to reserve their place in heaven.

The definition of "gospel" means absolute truth: something absolutely and unquestionably true. This is a tremendous gift we've been given. Of all the religions out there, this one offers an unshakeable foundation, one that we too would stake our lives on. If you were to ask any born-again Christian who is enjoying the fruits of being a child of God, if they would ever want to go back to their old life, I'll bet not one person would say yes. In these days of great uncertainty, where people feel the insecurity of the times unfolding, we have a job to do. We need to share the good news of the Gospel and offer our testimony no matter how many years we have been a Christian. May we have a new resolve and a great zeal to share the Good News today

Application

<u>Read</u>: Mark 16:15-20

<u>Pray</u>: Ask God to renew your joy and fill you with excitement in just being His child. Ask Him to help you share the Good News with someone today.

<u>Reflect</u>: Describe your conversion experience. Share it with someone today.

Day 29 - <u>A True Definition</u>

For the LORD your God is God of gods and Lord of lords, the great God, mighty and awesome, who shows no partiality and accepts no bribes.
Deuteronomy 10:17 NIV

A few years ago, the word "awesome" became a household word. Everyone seemed to be saying it, first from the young people and then older ones. People say it when they really like something or are pleased with something. They might say, "Isn't that an awesome sunset?" Or they say, "Isn't that an awesome restaurant?" They even refer to other people and say, "Isn't she awesome?" Or, "Wasn't that an awesome thing he did?"

But one day my husband and I were watching one of our favorite local (also national) Christian talk shows. The guest was a missionary with a well-known Christian missionary organization based in Hawaii. He commented that he disliked it when people used the word "awesome" other than when they were referring to God. In fact, he commented that only God deserves the word "awesome." Since then my husband and I try not to use the word unless we are talking about God or something God has done.

More recently, I read an article about the word "awesome." The writer said that there are other definitions for it, like awful and terrible. If you think about it, the word, "awful" really means "full of awe." So when we think of God, we are full of awe. The King James Version of the Bible uses the word "terrible" instead of awesome in the opening verse (Deut. 10:17). Terrible in this respect, means awe-inspiring, too great to even comprehend, magnificent and almost unspeakable in its greatness. All you have to do is go outside at night and take a look at the universe God created and remember you are only seeing a small part of it since the human eye can only see the stars and planets that are

Day 29

illuminated. There are billions more unseen to the human eye. Think of an evening when you stood outside and watched the Northern Lights dancing magically and mysteriously across the sky. Think of the heights of majestic mountains so high they are lost in the mist of the clouds.

To give you a better idea of how awesome God is, I'd like to share about something we read in a book that talked about the holiness of God. The author shared that in the Book of Revelation (see Rev. 4:8), it says that there are four living creatures who worship at the throne of God night and day without any rest. We wonder how they can do this, but they have a front row seat in God's marvellous presence and every time God reveals something more about Himself, they bow and worship. It is so awesome, they cry out, "Holy, Holy, Holy." In response to this, the Bible says that 24 elders fall down before God, worship Him and throw their crowns before God's throne. God is a holy God, so much so, that we can only wonder how or why He loves us so much. In light of this, to use the word "awesome" so loosely and as part of our every day language seems more like slang and an inappropriate use of a word that only belongs to God. May we use it respectfully and often in reference to our awesome and incredible God.

Application

Read: Revelation 4

Pray: Seek God for a glimpse and a revelation of His holiness. Ask Him to help guide you in a meditation of Scripture about His awesomeness.

Reflect: In what ways has God revealed His holiness to you? Write about it. Then spend some quiet time meditating on Scriptures that talk about the awesomeness of God. Use a Bible concordance if you have one or borrow one from a friend.

Day 30 - <u>Weather-Wise</u>

Dost thou know the balancings of the clouds, the wondrous works of him which is perfect in knowledge? Job 37:16

One day I was reading in Job about the clouds and how God uses weather to bring about His will. We may think that the clouds are just a result of nature randomly raining here and there or missing other parts of the earth creating a drought. We hear about hurricanes in the south Atlantic, or tropical storms kicking up waves and wind so high, they destroy property and some people can't escape its fierceness. In the early summer we hear of tornadoes, or perhaps even experience the effects of one.

One summer it seemed that a few tornadoes hit our province, which is unusual for this part of the continent. On a very hot June day, late in the afternoon, we were heading north out of the city and noticed how black the sky was to the west of us. As we were driving to the cottage, we kept the radio on and every couple of minutes a beep sounded and the radio announcer warned of a tornado and for anyone near certain areas to take immediate cover. Later, when we watched the news on TV, we learned that a tornado had touched down just 40 minutes west of where we had been driving. It had destroyed many homes and buildings in a small town, but miraculously, no one was seriously injured or killed. I read in the newspaper the next day that a family had been sitting in their basement praying for the safety of everyone, even as their home was being swept away. Truly God had protected people, since, at the time the tornado hit, most of the residents of the small town had been to a neighboring town attending a grade 12 graduation ceremony.

Then another series of tornadoes went through a popular resort area to the east of the city, ripping through the Whiteshell area destroying many homes and cottages. Then

Day 30

another series of tornadoes went further east into Ontario and destroyed many cottages in my sister's resort town. In fact, her cottage was damaged when a large tree fell on the rooftop. Again, God's hand was in it, since no one was at the cottage at the time.

While reading Job, I found an interesting verse:

He causeth it [the clouds] to come, whether for correction, or for his land, or for mercy. Job 37:13

According to this verse, God uses weather for His own purposes. We may be able to control many things, but only God can control the weather. This is His domain and He uses it for our good. He may use it to bring us in line with His will and perhaps to get our attention. He may use it to provide water for good crops, so that we can eat. Or He may use it to show mercy when rain is badly needed and we learn to trust Him to provide for all of our needs.

We are all interested in what the weather will be and no two days are ever exactly alike, at least, where we live. This keeps us on our toes and causes us to pray and trust God for the day and for our future. May we wisely consider the weather and what God may be trying to teach us.

Application

Read: Job 37

Pray: Ask God for His protection and provision in regards to the weather. Thank Him for always providing for your needs.

Reflect: Write about any weather stories you have experienced personally. How has God used weather in your life? Write about it.

An Invitation for Salvation

Dear Friend,

I hope this book has encouraged you. Daily devotions only truly benefit us once we've given our heart and entire life over to the Lord Jesus Christ. If you would like to receive Jesus into your heart and life today, and also have the assurance that you will spend eternity in heaven with Him, please begin by saying this prayer:

Dear Heavenly Father,

I come to you in the name of Jesus. Your Word says, "Whosoever shall call upon the name of the Lord shall be saved" (Acts 2:21). I call on you now and ask Jesus to come into my heart, forgive me for all my sins, and cleanse me. I ask you to be Lord over my life according to Romans 10:9-10 — "That if thou shalt confess with thy mouth the Lord Jesus, and shalt believe in thine heart that God hath raised him from the dead, thou shalt be saved. For with the heart man believeth unto righteousness; and with the mouth confession is made unto salvation." I do this now — I confess that Jesus is Lord and I believe in my heart that God raised Him from the dead.

In Jesus Name,
Amen

You are now reborn! You are a Christian and a child of God! Be assured, you have taken the most important step of your life and God has reserved your place in heaven. He will always be with you and lead you into all truth (read Hebrews 13:5b; John 14:26). You will need to read the Bible on a daily basis to get to know Him and all the many promises He has for you. As well, don't delay in contacting a Bible-believing church where you will find fellowship with others who have also taken this important life-changing step. May God bless you as you continue on your new path of life and freedom in Christ!

About the Author

Linda McBurney-Gunhouse enjoys her life in Manitoba, Canada. She writes to help others and inspire them to overcome difficulties and achieve success in life. She also enjoys story-telling in the form of writing fiction. Linda has spent a life-time writing and honing her skills. She studied Journalism, English, and History and received both a BA and B.Ed. in English. She has a diploma in magazine writing. She has worked as a contributing editor for a community college and also as an editor for a community newspaper in Winnipeg. Her articles have appeared in national, city and community newspapers and one magazine. She has written and sold one radio play. She is an accomplished eBook author of several inspirational books, including five full-length fiction. Her readership is international, and some of her eBooks frequently reach the Top 100 in specific categories. Linda also writes thought-provoking blogs.

She loves to share her faith and how she has overcome the many challenges in life in a way that readers can relate to. She sometimes teaches Creative Writing, and she does special speaking. She sometimes does free-lance writing for the local newspapers. She has also facilitated her own writer's group in a local setting. She continues to expand her thought-provoking blogs and book-writing. When she is not writing, she loves to be involved in creating several mediums of art.

Other Titles by Linda McBurney-Gunhouse

Inspirational Books

When Love Is All There Is
Loneliness: The Pathway to Discovery
Victory Over Backsliding
Footpath to Freedom
The Journey of Oneness
Power Thoughts for Positive Thinking
The Power of Submission
Healing For The Wounded Soul
The Act of Decision-Making
Cures for Stress
Freedom Through Spiritual Discernment
Spiritual Leadership in a Fallen World
The Journey to Contentment
No Fear of Hell
Money: Master or Servant?
The Bible: Conformed or Transformed?
Healing & Hope for Child Loss
Essential Steps to Increase Your Faith
Making Sense of the Rapture

Biography

The Bonk Saga: A History of Memories
Called to Overcome

Other Titles

Devotionals

Pathways to Devotion I
Pathways to Devotion II
Pathways to Devotion III
Pathways to Devotion IV
Pathways to Devotion V
Pathways to Devotion VI
Pathways to Devotion VII
Pathways to Devotion VIII
Pathways to Devotion IX
Pathways to Devotion X
Pathways to Devotion XI

Fiction

The Redemption of Steep Rock Cove
Return to Steep Rock Cove
Christmas Comes to Steep Rock Cove
Waves of Change at Steep Rock Cove
Driving with the Top Down
Track Three

Poetry Books

Heart Songs
Songs in the Desert
Water Crossings
Wings I: Morning Arising
Wings II: Daylight Reflections
Wings III: Contemplation

Other Titles

Creative How-to Books

Artistic Ideas & Inspirations
How to Create Stories From Your Own Life
Living a Creative Life

Writing Manuals

Creative Writing
Write Your Life Story
Fiction Writing

Please visit our website at www.creativefocus.ca to discover the many books from this list that are available as eBooks.

Note: If you have enjoyed reading this book, or any other eBook of mine, please rate it online, or recommend it on your Facebook page. It will help spread the word, and let others know it is available. My goal is to help, encourage and inspire others through my writing. Thank you and may God richly bless you!

www.ingramcontent.com/pod-product-compliance
Lightning Source LLC
Chambersburg PA
CBHW061341040426
42444CB00011B/3036